Let Freedom Ring

Kit Carson
Mountain Man

by Tracey Boraas

Consultant
Robert Moore, Historian
Jefferson National Expansion Memorial
St. Louis, Missouri

Bridgestone Books
an imprint of Capstone Press
Mankato, Minnesota

Bridgestone Books are published by Capstone Press
PO Box 669 • 151 Good Counsel Drive • Mankato, Minnesota 56002
http://www.capstone-press.com

Printed in the United States of America

Library of Congress Cataloging-in-Publication Data
Boraas, Tracey.
      Kit Carson: Mountain man/by Tracey Boraas.
           p. cm. — (Let Freedom Ring)
      Summary: Traces the life of the well-known figure from the Old West, Kit Carson, from his childhood in Kentucky and Missouri, through his years as a trapper, explorer and soldier, to his death in Colorado in 1868.
      Includes bibliographical references and index.
      ISBN 0-7368-1349-7 (hardcover)
      1. Carson, Kit, 1809–1868—Juvenile literature. 2. Pioneers—West (U.S.)—Biography—Juvenile literature. 3. Scouts and scouting—West (U.S.)—Biography—Juvenile literature. 4. Soldiers—West (U.S.)—Biography—Juvenile literature. 5. West (U.S.)—Biography—Juvenile literature. 6. Frontier and pioneer life—West (U.S.)—Juvenile literature. [1. Carson, Kit, 1809-1868. 2. Pioneers. 3. Soldiers. 4. Scouts and scouting. 5. West (U.S.)—History—19th century.] I. Title. II. Series.
      F592.C33 B67 2003
      978'.02'092—dc21
                                       2001007881

Editorial Credits

Charles Pederson, editor; Kia Adams, series designer and illustrator; Jennifer Schonborn and Juliette Peters, book designers; Kelly Garvin, photo researcher; Karen Risch, product planning editor

Photo Credits

Stock Montage, Inc., cover (middle), 5, 10; Stockbyte, cover (bottom left), 4, 12, 20, 28, 38; Hulton Deutsch Collection/CORBIS, 7 (left); PhotoSphere Images, 7 (right), 15 (right), 31 (right), 33 (right), 43; Charles Johnson, winner of the 2000 Lemelson-MIT High School Invention Apprenticeship/photo by Alan Borrud, courtesy of the Lemelson-MIT Program, 8 (bottom); CORBIS, 8 (top), 23, 33 (left); Kit Houghton/CORBIS, 9; courtesy of the Colorado Historical Society, 11; Underwood and Underwood/CORBIS, 13; North Wind Picture Archives, 15 (left); Hulton/Archive, 16; courtesy of Columbia River Knife & Tool, 17; from the collections of the Omaha Public Library, 19; courtesy of Elbert Edwards Collection, University of Nevada, Las Vegas, Library, 21; courtesy of Taos Historic Museums, 24, 29; the Society of California Pioneers, 30; Library of Congress, 31 (left); Denver Public Library, 34, 35, 36, 39, 40

1 2 3 4 5 6 07 06 05 04 03 02

Table of Contents

Chapter One

Kit's Boyhood

In the early 1800s, Lindsey Carson, his wife Rebecca, and their family lived in a cabin in Madison County, Kentucky. Ten children crowded their small home. Five of the children were from Lindsey's first marriage. The other five belonged to both Lindsey and Rebecca. Their 11th child, Christopher, was born late on Christmas Eve 1809. The Carson family eventually grew to include 14 children.

Early in Christopher's life, his family began calling him Kit. He carried this nickname his entire life. The short name fit his size. Christopher was a small child who remained small his entire life.

Before Kit was 2 years old, the Carson family moved to a farm near Franklin, Missouri. Daniel Boone had come to Missouri in the 1790s, and some stories say that the Carsons moved there to follow him. Kit admired Boone, who was growing old. From Boone, Kit learned to respect American Indians, as well as to hunt, track, and shoot.

The house Kit lived in as a child appears in this drawing.

Runaway Notice

Kit enjoyed the Workmans but ran away from them in 1826. David Workman's notice about Kit's disappearance read as follows:

"Notice is hereby given to all persons that CHRISTOPHER CARSON, a boy . . . small of his age, but thick set, light hair, ran away . . . on or about the first day of September . . . One cent reward will be given to any person who will bring back the said boy."
—*Missouri Intelligencer*, October 6, 1826

Troubled Years

In 1819, when Kit was age 9, a tree crushed and killed his father, Lindsey, as he cleared farmland. Four years later, Kit's mother remarried. Her new husband, Joseph Martin, brought several of his own children to the family.

Kit did not seem to like this new and even larger family. His behavior became hard to manage. First, his mother sent him to live with an older half brother, William. As Kit's behavior worsened, he was placed in the care of John Ryan, a future Missouri state supreme court judge.

Finally, Kit's family decided that he should learn a trade. They hoped he would then settle down. At age 15, Kit became an apprentice to David and William Workman. An apprentice learns a trade by working under the guidance of a skilled master. Kit learned the trade of saddlemaking. In the 1800s, saddlemaking was a valuable skill. Many people traveled by horse and needed skilled leatherworkers to make and maintain the equipment.

Experienced saddlemakers often hired young boys as apprentices to learn the trade by working on the job. This saddlemaker's photo was taken in 1953.

Apprentices Then and Now

In Kit's time, boys in their early teens were the usual

apprentices. An apprentice went to live with a skilled master of a trade. This person taught the boy and also fed, housed, and clothed him. In return, the boy worked for the master without pay for seven years. Once the training ended, the boy became a journeyman. He could work for any master who wanted him, or he could start his own business.

Today, the U.S. Bureau of Apprenticeship and Training oversees apprenticeship programs. These programs must include supervised work experience and classroom

training. Apprentices now receive pay with regular pay increases. The bureau sets standards for judging apprentice progress. When apprentices finish their training, they become journeyworkers.

The Workman shop was a natural gathering place for travelers moving west. As Kit worked quietly at his bench, he heard people tell stories about their travels. More than anything, Kit wanted to join the people who traveled the western trails. Even three of his brothers had become western settlers. But Kit felt stuck in the workshop. He liked David and William Workman but disliked his apprenticeship with them. He hated sitting all day at a workbench with a pile of leather and some tools.

Today's tools for saddlemaking are probably similar to those Kit used.

Runaway

Late in the summer of 1826, a wagon train began the long journey into Spanish territory. It would be the last train that year on the 800-mile (1,300-kilometer) Santa Fe Trail. Kit knew that if he did not act, he could not join another for many months. Taking only an old gun that had been his father's, Kit set out to catch the wagon train.

Wagon trains traveled the Santa Fe Trail when Kit was young.
He wanted to join one and head west.

Kit reached the wagons and convinced the train leader to give him a job. The leader hired Kit as a cavvy. His job was to herd the extra horses and mules needed for the long journey. At last, Kit was headed west.

In November 1826, Kit arrived in Santa Fe, in present-day New Mexico. He saw that David Workman had sent a public notice to the town stating that Kit had run away. It asked people to tell Workman if they saw him.

Workman did not seem too anxious to have Kit back. The law required masters to report runaway apprentices within 30 days after they disappeared. Workman waited the full 30 days before doing his legal duty. In addition, he offered only one penny as a reward for Kit's return. Kit believed that Workman understood Kit's need to be in the West.

Chapter Two

Mountain Man

In 1826, beaver hats were popular in the eastern United States and in Europe. Western mountain men trapped beavers to supply beaver pelts, or skins, for the hatmakers. Kit wanted to be one of these independent trappers and live in the mountains.

Trapping in the West could be dangerous. Wild animals could kill a trapper. American Indians sometimes attacked. The weather in the mountains could change in an instant from beautiful to deadly. Trappers often went into the mountains in the safety of organized groups.

No one in Santa Fe wanted to hire Kit for a trapping expedition. He was 16 and small for his age. He had too little experience to make him valuable to a trapping party.

From Santa Fe, Kit traveled north to the village of Taos. There, he met an old friend of his father named Kincaid. Kincaid was a retired trapper.

As a young man, Kit wanted to be a mountain man, but no one seemed to want him. He had too little trapping experience.

Kit spent the winter learning from the old mountain man. Kincaid taught Kit Spanish and several American Indian languages, including sign language. Kincaid taught Kit to make his own clothes from fur and animal skins. Kit learned to dry meat to make it last. Kincaid also taught Kit to respect American Indians.

Odd Jobs

In the spring of 1827, Kit was determined to reach the mountains, but he never got the chance. Finally, Kit took any jobs he could find. He cooked for Ewing Young of the Rocky Mountain Fur Company in Santa Fe. He interpreted Spanish for a group of businessmen on a trip into Mexico. He drove a team of horses for a copper-mining company. Kit returned to Taos each spring and fall.

Kit was disappointed not to become a trapper. But he was gaining the experience that he would need as a mountain man. He was becoming an excellent horseman and marksman. He learned to be alert to the dangers of desert travel. He became familiar with waterless marches. He recognized places where American Indians might attack.

A Chance at Last

Each spring and fall, Kit tried to join a trapping party. In August 1829, Kit was left behind again as each group left Taos. He did not know how he would make it through another winter. He made a difficult decision to sell his father's gun to Ewing Young.

At Young's business, a party of trappers had just returned. Apache Indians had robbed the season's catch of furs. They also had stripped and made fun of

Kit stood next to his horse in this drawing. He wore his trapper's clothing.

Fur Trading

The American fur trade lasted until the mid-1800s. Beavers had the most valuable fur. Beaver fur was used to make hats such as the one at right. By the 1830s, beavers were becoming scarce from heavy trapping. Instead of beaver hats, silk hats became popular in Europe and the United States. The value of beaver fur dropped sharply. This drop brought an end to the era of the trapper.

the trappers. Young decided to lead the next trapping party himself. He wanted to prove that the Apaches could not keep his men from the mountains.

Kit approached Young to offer him the gun. Young said he needed the man behind the gun more than he needed the gun. Young was determined to trap for furs in Apache territory and wanted Kit to join the group. Kit took a skinning knife, sharpening stone, warm blanket, gunpowder, and lead for ammunition. He rode from Taos with Young and a group of about 40 men.

To California

Young's trappers were careful. They never hunted alone. At night, they tied their horses so the Apache could not easily drive them off. Still, the Apache were able to kill some of the trappers' pack animals. They were not able to trap many animals.

Young decided to trap somewhere more dangerous than Apache territory. He would take his team across the western Mojave Desert and into California. Water and animals were scarce. More than half of the trappers refused to go. Kit was the first man to agree to the dangerous journey.

The modern Kit Carson knife is fashioned after Kit's own design.

Kit, Young, and the remaining men prepared to cross the desert. They hunted for food but shot only three deer. They made the deerskins into containers to carry water.

Young's men were soon deep in the desert. Each man received only a small amount of water at the end of each day. Someone guarded the water to make sure no one took more than his share. The mules had no food or water. With earlier wagon trains, Kit had learned to continue in the worst conditions. Now he led the men and mules forward.

The men struggled for four days before finding water. After resting and drinking, the group again marched into the desert. After another four days, Kit led the staggering men and animals to the banks of the Colorado River. They were able to buy a horse from the Mojave Indians, which they cooked and ate. They continued west and finally arrived at the valleys of California. There, they successfully hunted and trapped for three years.

A Real Mountain Man

When Kit returned to Taos in 1831, he had traveled 3,000 miles (5,070 kilometers). He proved his

Waanibe

In 1834, Kit married a woman named Waanibe. She was an Arapaho Indian who may have dressed in a fashion similar to the woman shown here. Waanibe died after giving birth to their second child.

leadership during those years. He memorized the areas in which he had traveled and became familiar with much of the West.

For the next 10 years, Kit hunted and trapped from Montana to New Mexico. He roamed the mountains, learning the passes, streams, lakes, and valleys. He became familiar with the Midwest and the Northwest. He became known as "The King of the Mountain Men."

Within a few years, beaver hats went out of fashion. The price of beaver furs quickly fell. The time of the mountain men had passed.

Chapter Three

The Frémont Expeditions

Kit returned to New Mexico. The trading company of Bent and St. Vrain offered Kit a job supplying meat for the people living at Bent's Fort, in present-day Colorado. Kit was an excellent hunter. He could ride his horse into a thundering buffalo herd and kill an animal with a single shot.

Kit became the fort's chief hunter. Other people were hired to help him. He earned $500 a month from November through March. Sometimes, he rode as a messenger, delivering messages between wagon trains and Taos or Santa Fe.

In 1837, Kit's first daughter, Adaline, was born. In 1840, Waanibe died after delivering her second daughter. No one knows what happened to this baby.

In 1842, Kit returned for the first time to his family in Missouri. He left Adaline with his sister Mary Ann. Kit then boarded

Kit (standing) and John Charles Frémont (seated) were scouts and explorers. They were also good friends.

a steamship for St. Louis. On the ship, he met John Charles Frémont. This man was part of Kit's life for the next several years.

Joining Frémont

On the boat trip to St. Louis, Kit and Frémont spoke about Frémont's goals. He wanted to make a map of the area along the Oregon Trail from St. Louis to the Rocky Mountains. He had hired men back in St. Louis, but he lacked a good guide for the journey. Kit knew the areas Frémont was to explore. He offered himself as a guide.

On June 10, 1842, Kit led Frémont's first expedition west. The group consisted of 28 men. Their goal was to explore the Oregon Trail from St. Louis to South Pass in the Rocky Mountains. With Kit as his guide, John's group safely explored and mapped the Oregon Trail to the Wind River Mountains in present-day Wyoming.

Return to Bent's Fort

Kit returned to Bent's Fort in the fall of 1842. He again began to deliver messages across the plains to Taos. Skilled at wilderness survival, he was the only

Frémont Peak

John Frémont and some of his party climbed what he thought was the tallest peak in the Rocky Mountains. He named it Frémont Peak. Pictured below, Frémont heroically plants the U.S. flag in the Wind River Mountain range of the Rockies.

man who could be counted on to pass through unfriendly American Indian lands. If war parties blocked him, he might hide during the day. Then at night, he could slip past the Indians.

In Taos, Kit met a young Mexican woman named Josefa Maria Jaramillo. Josefa was not quite 15 years old when she married the 34-year-old Kit in February 1843. Kit promptly sent for Adaline to join them. He often was separated from his family, but his daughter had a new home and stepmother.

Josefa Jaramillo married Kit Carson in 1843. She became stepmother to Kit's daughter Adaline.

Frémont's Second Expedition

In 1843, Kit joined Frémont's second expedition through the vast territory west of the Rocky Mountains. The explorers set out from St. Louis. They crossed present-day Colorado, then headed northwest through present-day Wyoming. They continued through southern Idaho, making a trip south to map the Great Salt Lake area. They turned north again through Oregon to the Columbia River.

From the Columbia River, Frémont's group turned south. People in the area said that crossing the Sierra Nevada mountains in winter was dangerous. Frémont ignored these people and started the journey. The group wanted to reach Sutter's Fort in the valley of the Sacramento River of California.

Again Kit found himself leading people through danger. The snow was deep, food ran low, and the men were exhausted. Many of them became ill. The men killed and ate some of their animals. Kit pushed the expedition through a high mountain pass in the Sierra Nevadas. The struggling men made their final push into the Sacramento Valley.

Claiming the West

In the mid-1800s, the United States wanted to challenge Great Britain's claim to the Pacific Northwest. It also wanted to challenge Mexico's claim to the American Southwest. The U.S. government sent Frémont to explore and map these western areas. With accurate maps and reports, the government could encourage U.S. citizens to move to these areas. Having large numbers of settlers in these areas would give the U.S. government a good claim to them. Frémont's expeditions helped the government's plan.

Frémont's men rested at Sutter's Fort to regain their health. Then they set out again. This time they crossed the Mojave Desert northeast through Utah. Curving back through Colorado, the expedition reached St. Louis in 1844.

In one year, Kit had led Frémont's men more than 5,500 miles (8,850 kilometers). In the official report of his expedition, Frémont included many examples of Kit's skill, bravery, and loyalty. Thousands of copies of the report sold quickly, and Kit became famous almost overnight.

BRITISH TERRITORY

U.S. TERRITORY

Missouri River

Sutter's Fort

SIERRA NEVADA RANGE

Great Salt Lake

ROCKY MOUNTAINS

Fort Garland

Bent's Fort

Taos

Santa Fe

San Diego

PACIFIC OCEAN

MEXICAN TERRITORY

El Paso

Legend
— Mexican Border
▨ British Territory
▢ U.S. Territory
▢ Mexican Territory
---- Santa Fe Trail
- - - Oregon Trail
● City
★ Capital City
⚲ Fort

Scale
Miles
0   50   100   150   200
0   100   200   300
Kilometers

N
W   E
S

Mexican Territory in 1830

Chapter Four

Western Wars

In the early 1800s, many white Americans believed it was their right to expand their country's borders westward into new lands. This belief was called Manifest Destiny. In 1845, as part of Manifest Destiny, the U.S. Congress voted to annex, or take control of, Texas from Mexico. But that was not enough. The U.S. government wanted to expand its territory all the way to the Pacific Ocean.

In the 1840s, California was a Mexican state with its own government. In 1841, the first organized group of American settlers came overland to California. These settlers wanted California to become part of the United States. But Mexico refused to give up the land.

The Mexican War

In 1845, Frémont led a third western expedition. His mission was to encourage the people in California to fight Mexican

Kit served as a military officer first in the U.S. Civil War (1861–1865) and later in the wars against American Indian nations.

Did You Know?

William Todd designed the flag created for the U.S. settlers' battle efforts. Todd was a nephew of Mary Todd Lincoln, Abraham Lincoln's wife. The flag had a red star and a grizzly bear on a white background.

control. Kit guided Frémont's party across the western mountains and deserts to California.

The Mexicans did not trust Frémont. This distrust occurred because his party was made up of U.S. soldiers. Frémont himself was an army officer.

In March 1846, the Mexicans ordered Frémont to move his troops out of California. Instead, Frémont marched to Monterey, California's capital at that time. He began to build a fort there.

On May 13, 1846, Congress declared war on Mexico. This began the Mexican War (1846–1848). In June 1846, Frémont led U.S. settlers in the fight against the Mexican government in California.

In September, Frémont gave Kit messages to deliver to President James Polk. Kit left with 15 men for the 3,000-mile (4,800-kilometer) trip to Washington, D.C.

At the same time, U.S. Army General Stephen Kearny marched his troops west from Fort Leavenworth, Kansas. He planned to capture New Mexico. Kit met Kearny at Socorro, New Mexico. Kearny ordered Kit to lead his soldiers across the desert to California. Kit never delivered his messages to the president.

RECRUITING
OFFICE,
COMPANY B,
SCOTT LEGION REGIMENT,
COL. S. W. BLACK,
Late Col. of 1st Penn. Reg., Mexican War.
TO BE MUSTERED IN IMMEDIATELY.
Capt. JAMES F. HEFLEY.

Posters invited men to serve as soldiers in the U.S. Army during the Mexican War.

On December 6, Mexican soldiers attacked Kearny's troops near San Diego, California. Kearny sent Kit and navy Lieutenant Edward Beale to bring U.S. soldiers from San Diego. During the night, Kit and Beale removed their shoes and sneaked past the Mexican Army. The men crawled over rocks and around brush, close to Mexican soldiers. Then, losing their shoes, they walked barefoot for the remaining 30 miles (48 kilometers) to San Diego.

Kit and Beale's efforts saved Kearny's army. Soldiers immediately left San Diego to help Kearny. By January 1847, troops under Kearny and U.S. Commodore Robert Stockton had completed the U.S. victory in California. Kit was appointed a lieutenant in the army.

The Mexican War ended in 1848. As part of the settlement, the United States paid Mexico about $15 million for California, New Mexico, and other areas of the Southwest.

Indian Agent

In 1853, Kit was named as an agent to the southwestern Apache, Ute, and Pueblo peoples of New Mexico. He represented the U.S. government.

He spoke the languages of these people. They regarded him as an honest and fair man.

Kit realized that these people could no longer provide for themselves as they once had. The number of wild animals was falling due to white settlement. Kit said the U.S. government either could "… clothe them [the American Indians] or exterminate [kill] them." He suggested that the Indians who relied on hunting should be taught instead to farm. That way, they could provide their own food.

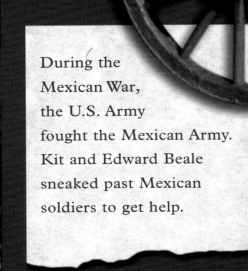

During the Mexican War, the U.S. Army fought the Mexican Army. Kit and Edward Beale sneaked past Mexican soldiers to get help.

The Wars against American Indians

The Apache were unwilling to become farmers and began to attack settlers. Kit met with the Apache to talk about peace. They did not harm him because they respected him. But after he left, they began their attacks again.

When peace failed, Kit led U.S. soldiers to track down the tribes, defeat them, and send them

Representatives of many American Indian nations met in Washington, D.C., to sign the Kit Carson Treaty of 1868.

Kit's Communication

Kit's government position required much paperwork, although he had never learned to read or write. A clerk named John Mostin helped him take care of government reports. But Kit knew how to communicate in the languages of the Navajo, Apache, Comanche, Cheyenne, Arapaho, Crow, Blackfeet, Shoshone, Paiute, and Ute. The Cheyenne scout Viejo (right) served with Kit in the Indian wars of 1855.

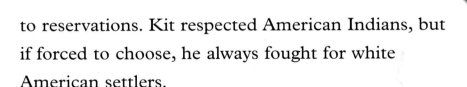

to reservations. Kit respected American Indians, but if forced to choose, he always fought for white American settlers.

In early 1861, the Civil War (1861–1865) broke out between the Northern and Southern United States. Kit resigned as Indian agent to join the Northern army. He was appointed lieutenant colonel of the New Mexico Volunteer Regiment. In 1862, Kit led his troops against Southern forces at Valverde, New Mexico.

The Navajo, Apache, Comanche, Cheyenne, and Ute saw the war as an opportunity to reclaim their land. While the North and South battled each other, the tribes began to attack settlers again.

Kit received orders to stop the attack. In the fall of 1862, he tracked down the attackers and

Navajo warriors like these fought hard to keep their people from being forced to live on reservations.

successfully forced hundreds of Apache onto a reservation. After that, most of the remaining tribes stopped their attacks.

The Navajo Holdouts

The Navajo did not want to live on reservations. This was the strongest of the southwest tribes. They attacked settlers in present-day northern New Mexico and Arizona. They raided farms, killed settlers, stole animals, and burned buildings. They ignored U.S. soldiers and moved north toward present-day Colorado and Utah.

In late 1862, General James H. Carleton ordered Kit to burn Navajo fields and kill Navajo animals. These actions would leave the Navajo without food for the winter. Kit followed Carleton's orders and defeated the Navajo. He forced 8,000 Navajo to walk 300 miles (480 kilometers) from Arizona to a New Mexico reservation.

Kit had won the war against the Indian nations, but he was unhappy in his victory. In a letter to Josefa, Kit said, "I can take no pride in this fearful destruction . . . My sleep is haunted by dreams of starving Navajo women and children."

Chapter Five

Final Years

For nearly five years, Kit led soldiers against American Indians. But he was growing tired from years of fighting. In 1866, Kit became commanding general of a force of 1,000 men at Fort Garland, Colorado. He was ordered to keep peace between the Ute, Apache, and U.S. settlers. Kit sold his home in Taos and moved his family to Colorado.

In October 1867, Kit received a permanent injury. As Kit inspected land around the fort, his horse threw him and knocked him unconscious. Kit's heart also was damaged. There was no treatment for Kit's heart condition. He retired from the military and moved to Fort Lyon, Colorado, near the site of Bent's Fort.

Josefa and Kit Die

In April 1868, Josefa gave birth to the Carsons' seventh child. But it was a difficult birth,

In the last years of Kit's life, he grew tired of war. When his heart was injured in an accident, Kit had to retire from military service.

and Josefa did not recover. She died on April 23, 1868. Her death deeply affected Kit.

Kit's condition worsened. He took medicine to control the pain. On May 23, 1868, Kit died. He was buried with military honors next to Josefa. Months later, Josefa and Kit's bodies were removed from their Colorado graves and reburied in Taos.

Remembering Kit

People's idea of heroism changes as the world changes. Today, many people see Kit as a man who

Kit's gravestone marks the spot in Taos, New Mexico, where he received his final burial.

Kit and American Indians

Kit wanted to help Indians live in a land that was no longer theirs. A man named James Rusling met Kit at Fort Garland. Rusling described Kit as a kind and generous friend of the American Indians. According to Rusling, Kit said that "bad white men" had caused the problems with American Indians. Rusling added that "Carson pleaded [argued] for the Indians . . . whom we were daily robbing of their hunting grounds and homes." Rusling quoted Kit saying, "What der yer 'spose our Heavenly Father, who made both them and us, thinks of [the way we have treated American Indians]?"

murdered American Indians. But Kit was a man of his time. He fought for whites when he had to choose between them and American Indians. Yet, he did his best to help Indian nations.

Across the country, people knew Kit as a guardian of the West and a protector of settlers. He promoted westward expansion. He guided expeditions through unsettled areas. He was a trapper, hunter, Indian agent, and brave fighter.

TIMELINE

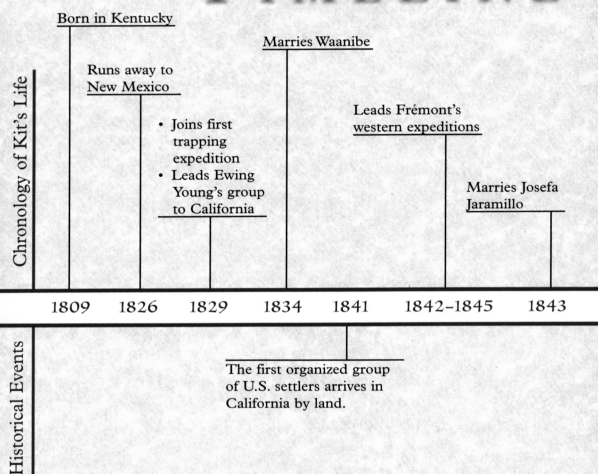

Chronology of Kit's Life

Born in Kentucky

Runs away to New Mexico

Marries Waanibe

- Joins first trapping expedition
- Leads Ewing Young's group to California

Leads Frémont's western expeditions

Marries Josefa Jaramillo

| 1809 | 1826 | 1829 | 1834 | 1841 | 1842–1845 | 1843 |

Historical Events

The first organized group of U.S. settlers arrives in California by land.

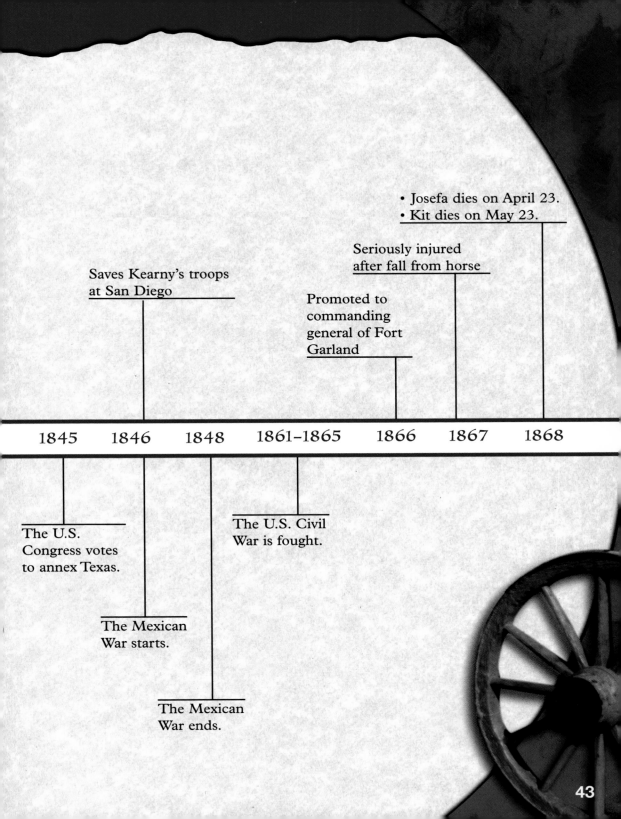

• Josefa dies on April 23.
• Kit dies on May 23.

Seriously injured
after fall from horse

Saves Kearny's troops
at San Diego

Promoted to
commanding
general of Fort
Garland

| 1845 | 1846 | 1848 | 1861–1865 | 1866 | 1867 | 1868 |

The U.S.
Congress votes
to annex Texas.

The U.S. Civil
War is fought.

The Mexican
War starts.

The Mexican
War ends.

Glossary

ambush (AM-bush)—to hide and then attack someone

apprentice (uh-PREN-tiss)—someone who learns a trade or craft by working with a skilled person

cavvy (KAV-ee)—a person who worked on a wagon train to herd the extra horses and mules throughout the journey

Confederate (kuhn-FED-ur-uht)—a person who banded together with others in the South to oppose the North during the Civil War

expedition (ek-spuh-DISH-uhn)—a long journey for a purpose such as exploring

pelt (PELT)—an animal's skin with the hair or fur still on it

reservation (rez-ur-VAY-shuhn)—an area of land set aside for a special purpose such as a home for American Indians

For Further Reading

Boekhoff, P. M., and Stuart A. Kallen. *California.* Seeds of a Nation. San Diego, Calif.: Kidhaven Press, 2001.

Bruchac, Joseph. *Navajo Long Walk: The Tragic Story of a Proud People's Forced March from Their Homeland.* Washington, D.C.: National Geographic Society, 2002.

Burger, James P. *Mountain Men of the West.* The Library of the Western Expansion. New York: PowerKids Press, 2002.

Calvert, Patricia. *The American Frontier.* Great Lives. New York: Atheneum Books for Young Readers, 1997.

Graves, Kerry A. *The Civil War.* America Goes to War. Mankato, Minn.: Capstone Books, 2001.

Witteman, Barbara. *John Charles Frémont: Western Pathfinder.* Let Freedom Ring. Mankato, Minn.: Bridgestone Books, 2003.

Places of Interest

Bent's Old Fort National Historic Site

35110 Highway 194 East
La Junta, CO 81050-9523

Bent's Old Fort re-creates the grounds and buildings that Kit knew as a trapper.

Fort Garland Museum

29477 Highway 159
P.O. Box 368
Fort Garland, CO 81133

The museum re-creates the fort Kit commanded in the 1860s.

Kit Carson Home and Museum

113 Kit Carson Road
Taos, NM 87571

The museum is in Kit's Taos home. It has furnished period rooms, mountain man relics, and gun displays.

Santa Fe Trail Center

Route 3
Larned, Kansas 67550

Visitors can learn about the Santa Fe Trail through indoor and outdoor exhibits.

Internet Sites

Christopher Houston "Kit" Carson: Authentic Legend of the Desert Southwest
http://www.desertusa.com/mag99/jan/papr/kitcarson.html
Visitors can read a brief outline of Kit's life.

Death of Kit Carson
http://pages.prodigy.com/legends/kcarson.htm
The site contains a brief account of Kit's life and death, from the *Rocky Mountain News* newspaper, Wednesday, May 27, 1868.

Fort Garland Museum
http://www.museumtrail.org/FortGarlandMuseum.asp
Viewers can see photos and information on this fort that Kit commanded.

The Mountain Men: Pathfinders of the West, 1810–1860
http://xroads.virginia.edu/~HYPER/HNS/Mtmen/home.html
Viewers can learn about the American fur trade and about the mountain men.

New Perspectives on the West: Kit Carson
http://www.pbs.org/weta/thewest/people/a_c/carson.htm
This site has information on Kit and his life.

Index